PRAISE FOR JACQUELINE PIRTLE

Jacqueline takes you always directly to what you are ready to see or experience.

— LONGTIME CLIENT AND READER

It is liberating to face your own blocks and to be finally free of the weight that they have caused for many years. And while for me the changes I'm experiencing are noticeable and real, I still feel like myself. Just a more sure self.

— LONGTIME CLIENT AND READER

Jacqueline makes me BELIEVE I can be and live a joyful and magical existence every new day of my life!

— LONGTIME CLIENT AND READER

JACQUELINE PIRTLE

OPEN

Where it all starts!

THE EXTENDED EDITION

COPYRIGHT

Copyright © 2021 Jacqueline Pirtle
www.FreakyHealer.com

All rights reserved. No part of this book may be reproduced or transmitted in any form or by any means, electronic or mechanical, including photocopying, recording, or by any information storage and retrieval system without the written permission of the publisher, except where permitted by law.

ISBN-13: 978-1-955059-09-1

Publisher: Freaky Healer

Editor-in-chief: Zoe Pirtle
All-round Support: Mitch Pirtle

Book cover design by Kingwood Creations kingwoodcreations.com

Author photo courtesy of Lionel Madiou madious.com

I want to let you know that all my books and holistic practitioner work together are a wholesome system, supporting you to live a more conscious, mindful, and happier life.

However, I made it so you can receive the benefit of living more joyously solely by working through this terrific journal book, while also experiencing the full satisfaction in continuing on to the next journal of this series—not to mention the rock solid tools you get by reading any of my other books or adding in my podcast *The Daily Freak*. Either way, I know you'll love my inspirational teachings.

Find out more:
www.freakyhealer.com
Amazon Author Page
The Daily Freak Podcast

So before you dive in, I want to thank you for hopping on the magic train with me! I truly hope you enjoy **Open** as much as I loved writing it, and if you do, it would be wonderful if you could take a short minute and leave a review on Amazon.com and Goodreads.com as soon as you can.

Your kind feedback helps other readers find my books easier, and be happy faster. Consider it a happy deed for the world.

Thank you!

ACKNOWLEDGMENTS

Let's be honest here... I have a dream team!

I could not have finished this book without the help of talented, creative, high-for-life, and phenomenal professionals.

From the bottom of my heart, I want to thank Zoe Pirtle for her editorial mastery; Mitch Pirtle for his all-round support; kingwoodcreations.com for their fun and polished book cover design; and madiouART.com for an amazing photo shoot.

I'd also like to extend a huge "Thank You!" to all the fans of my work and books—I created this beautiful journal series for you.

Life is spectacular with you on my side!

*If you ever wondered what would change for you if you were to BE and live **open** to the full extent of experiencing a vivid life, then you came to the right place!*

"I got you covered," says this journal book!

DEDICATION

*I dedicate this journal to all **closed** beings or things and challenge them to become **open**!*

INTRODUCTION

Incredible *open-uppers*,

I'm over the moon happy to be on this journey with you - connected and together - to mindfully and consciously create a better life for yourself and others—since you share your well-feeling with everything and everyone at all times. Just think of the power you have!

Everything is energy - you, me, this journal, your *open-ness*, and also *your closed-ness* - it's all one and the same: Energy!

It's also all connected and sharing at all times—meaning that you, your *blockages* and what they represent, and also the *open-ness* you will create with this journal, are all *one* and part of your wonderful being.

As these energies, everything, and everyone vibrates in different frequencies. Some are high like being **open**, and some are lower like being closed-up.

When you are **open** you are in a high value frequency because you go with the **open** flow of life and feel good since that essence represents living freely, forward, and resistance-free. In that *open-ness* is where you can truly be you, hear your inner guidance clearly, and can make your wishes, dreams, and desires come true.

Focusing on being *open* while dreaming about unlimited possibilities and thinking and feeling your dreams vividly - as alive - is a spectacular way of being.

In comparison, when you put all focus on your traumatic experiences that you have had, you are vibrating in a lower frequency because trauma feels like pain, sadness, anger, unhappiness, resentment, disbelief, and somewhat being unfortunate in life—clearly a state of being *closed* to well-being.

Sure, you can dwell on your hold-ups in life and get all deep into the *why* and *what*, letting them keep a tight grip on you and your life, but you can also take another road and shift your focus to your aligned *open-ness* while giving that magic the energetic momentum.

Know that you have the capability to get these closed patches so incredibly wide open - turning them inside out into an *openness* you never knew is possible - and feeling amazing by enjoying a healing of immense proportion.

Being **open** to all that life has in store for you is **where it all starts** because it allows unlimited opportunities to arrive in that wideness, since they can catch a hold of you until you hear - or sense - them loud and clear. Just think of that incredible match-up and shift into the higher frequency of happiness by being *one* with the excitement of these opportunities and manifestations. It's an automatic shot into being and living the best version of you—while changing at a constant and vivid speed, the way life naturally happens.

I say replace your *closed-ness* with your undeniable *open-ness* —boldly and widely living your life fully!

Journaling through this 90 day journal - the extended edition - of **Open** will bring huge change by creating exactly *that* open space, where new magic can BE for you.

For every day in this book, there is a profound *opening* entry,

INTRODUCTION

inviting you to shift yourself into feeling amazing by journaling about your thoughts—creating a huge wide essence of love, peace, happiness, appreciation, respect, gratitude, acceptance for yourself, your life, and your truth which you will share with everything and everyone.

You will feel your utmost excitement and awe of everything being possible—of you being deserving and in charge of how your life IS and unfolds and what's included or excluded fully. Plus you will become a master in feeling phenomenal and manifesting what you want, all while learning to open up, live more consciously and mindfully, and become happier. A change that is forever!

As a side note, there are a couple bonus days at the end; in case you ever find the need to do two in a day, or to keep working while you wait for the next journal in this series to arrive. I also left you a few blank *Open-ness IS* pages to journal about additional ways to open yourself to your deepest wishes and dreams as they come in and up for you.

Enough chit-chat, I know you are ready, so grab your pen and have incredible fun with catching more life than you have ever caught, in your new open ways.

Happiest,
    Jacqueline

# Day 1

IMAGINE A BEAUTIFUL, wide, tall, gigantic door with the most gorgeous handle that you have ever seen. What's the visual you get—what color is your door and what shape is the handle? Now see yourself standing in front of that incredibly exciting door, grabbing that magic handle, and without any expectations - rather, simply in wonder - opening this spectacular wide portal. Wow! What an experience! Feel your curiosity of what's behind. Do you have goose-bumps yet? Can you feel the wide opening of yourself to whatever this practice has in store for you—the opening shift, the exciting energy, and the unlimited possibilities that could be? Go on, this is your cue to put into words what this opening act means for you! Most importantly, focus only on the aperture, don't head through the door yet, because tomorrow you'll continue the journey into what's beyond your magical door.

Open - Where it all starts!

 ay 2

WELCOME back to your magnificent door, that you opened wide and big—to be specific, you are at the exact split-second when the door is opening and you are in wonder of what's behind. Feel your whole being - your physical body, mind, soul, and your consciousness - opening up, just like that door. Now step through that open portal into your new open space! Breathe into the excitement and in-aweness of what you see on the other side. What's there in your magic world? How do you feel being there? What and who do you want in this new open space of yours? What magic is waiting and asking for your attention?

_____
_____
_____
_____
_____
_____
_____
_____
_____
_____
_____
_____
_____
_____
_____
_____
_____

Open - Where it all starts!

 ay 3

Now that you have taken the leap through your fantastic door and are living in your wide open essence, it's time to acknowledge that everything and everyone in your life - the good, bad, beautiful, and ugly, as we so wonderfully say - are always a chance to open up even more; to your magic, healing, betterment, expansion, and calibration into being and living the higher version of you. Knowing this, what will change for you? How will you live differently? What are your expectations for yourself and others when living focused on everything always being a gift?

_____
_____
_____
_____
_____
_____
_____
_____
_____
_____
_____
_____
_____
_____
_____
_____

Open - Where it all starts!

Day 4

IN ORDER TO keep expanding beyond what you opened up to in the last few journal entries, we need to talk about what further open-ness is to you? How does it look, feel, sound, taste, and smell? What thoughts match it? What activities or practices represent you being more open? What words are you newly going to use and what lifestyle equals being more open?

_____
_____
_____
_____
_____
_____
_____
_____
_____
_____
_____
_____
_____
_____
_____
_____
_____
_____
_____
_____
_____

Open - Where it all starts!

 ay 5

To get you the clarity of the difference between you being wide open or closed, we need to put a small little spotlight onto what being closed feels like for you. So without going too deep into the negative or state of unwell-feeling, what does it mean to be closed? How does it feel when you are closed? Where in your life, body, emotions, or mind, do you feel such a closed sensation? How will you rip it open and also have it stay open?

___
___
___
___
___
___
___
___
___
___
___
___
___
___
___
___
___
___
___
___

Open - Where it all starts!

Day 6

AN OPEN HEART IS A ____ heart! Fill in the blank with a positive flair, then feel and breathe into your heart. Sense it opening up, letting your humongous love flow out and in, while opening wider and wider. How does this feel? What kind of new day, and life, will this open heart practice create for you? Are you smiling yet?

Open - Where it all starts!

 ay 7

OPEN UP TO YOUR FORCES! What does that look like for you? How do your forces feel? What are your forces? Pick some you would like to open up to. What do your forces do for your life, body, mind, soul, and for the world?

___

Open - Where it all starts!

 ay 8

IN ORDER TO get what you want, you need to be open and allow what you want to come skipping through the door of life. What is the one thing right now that you desperately wish for? How will you open up to allow this dream of yours to arrive? Hint—copy and paste that practice on to the next, and then the next, thing that you are dreaming of!

_____

Open - Where it all starts!

 Day 9

AN OPEN MIND IS A ___ mind! Fill in the blank with what fits for you. What thoughts that you have feel closed to you being happy, healthy, energized, and vivid? What is the opposite of those closed thoughts—the open version of them? Make your list and add how you feel when shifting like that!

Open - Where it all starts!

 ay 10

LITTLE MESSAGES, signs, and wisdom are always available for you. Some are big and bold and in your face, while others are tiny and more hidden—but they are never not there. How will you open yourself to consciously catch all that help while you can, and while they are there? What's your magic trick?

Open - Where it all starts!

 ay 11

FOR SOLUTIONS TO come in and up you have to be open to receive and allow them to be. List the problems, hardships, or issues that are on your mind—refrain from digging deep here. How can you open up to the goodness in those happenings? How can you allow the invitation for change to happen in your life openly? How will you open up here?

_____
_____
_____

Open - Where it all starts!

Day 12

AN OPEN BODY IS A ___ body! Fill in the blank and feel into your physical body, into its energy. Where do you catch closed-up patches, blockages? Is there any pain, sadness, anger, or gunky energy somewhere? How will you shift those locked gates to be wide open portals to health, energy, and well-being?

___

Open - Where it all starts!

 ay 13

Your heart wants you to open up to its guidance and to what it has to say—without ever questioning it. How will you openly and trustingly follow your heart more often?

Open - Where it all starts!

 ay 14

OPENING up to all your feelings - and not only loving the ones you like - means you allow yourself to be wholesome and complete, also as-is. How loving of you! What feelings are you already welcoming with open arms, and which ones not? How will you change that?

___

Open - Where it all starts!

 ay 15

To let go of all your unfitting and old beliefs you have to be open enough to let them disappear—because if you are closed, they will stay behind a locked door. What old habits are you wanting to "poof" be gone? How will you open up and let them fly away?

___

Open - Where it all starts!

 ay 16

CONGRATULATIONS, you have done quite some shifting so far! From this new open-ness, what does an open alignment with who you really are look like now? I bet it is very different than when you started your journey with *Open*. How will you stand up for this newfound you and *BE and live* as such?

_____
_____
_____
_____
_____
_____
_____
_____
_____
_____
_____
_____
_____
_____
_____
_____
_____
_____
_____
_____
_____
_____

Open - Where it all starts!

 ay 17

LIVING a full life means that you spread your wings wide and far —welcomingly embracing everything that is there for you at all times. This asks for your full trust, because having only half the trust gets you only half the adventure. How will you openly receive your life in its full bloom? What activities, inspirations, and flavors are involved in such a wondrous lifestyle?

Open - Where it all starts!

 ay 18

Do you like change? If yes, what kind of change would feel good right now? How will you open up so it can actually arrive? If no, what's blocking you to allow a shift—and how will you get your behind into an open-ness where different can be?

Open - Where it all starts!

 ay 19

CATCH your closed-up patches - your blockages - right now! Feel and sense into your physical body, your thoughts and feelings, your life, and your energy. Where are they—is there any physical symptom, emotional distress, or energetic impurity present? How will you shift those tight essences to be wide open again —*again* because once upon a time, they were?

_____
_____
_____
_____
_____
_____
_____
_____
_____
_____
_____
_____
_____
_____
_____
_____
_____
_____
_____

Open - Where it all starts!

 ay 20

YOU KNOW that crazy and unexplained inner voice of yours? Can you hear it? What is it saying? It takes your full open-ness to listen and follow its wisdom without ever questioning it. Are you that open? Are you that crazy? I hope I hear a "Yes!" Now how are you going to make sure that you stay that attentive?

Open - Where it all starts!

 ay 21

ARE you fully open to love? I'm not just talking about finding the love of your life—or having already found it. I'm bringing up the the essence, the energy, the feeling of love that is in your heart. Are you freely allowing the whole potential of love to flow through you? Are you willingly, and in a super-human style, ripping your chest open to welcome all love? Take a moment of reflection and write about how your incredible love feels for you, and what it is capable of! What is your letting-in-love plan?

_____
_____
_____
_____
_____
_____
_____
_____
_____
_____
_____
_____
_____
_____
_____
_____
_____

Open - Where it all starts!

 ay 22

BEING open to new ways of nourishing your physical body means that you are keeping up with your ever changing physics. What foods are not really fitting anymore? What new foods, fresh cuisine, and different tastes could you give a try? Or is it the timing and amounts that could use a change-up?

___

Open - Where it all starts!

 ay 23

MONEY! It's a gift from the heavens until it brings up negative, unhelpful, and downing feelings. Isn't that so? It takes lots of open-ness to allow the bounty of gold to arrive in unlimited fashion—because just like a shut door or one with only a peep-hole, not much will get through if you are closed. It also takes a loving attitude towards money because why else would money want to meet up with you? How are you going to manage a high-for-life attitude towards abundance—and how will you make sure you stay that way?

___

Open - Where it all starts!

 Day 24

Everything is always present in life; the negative and the positive, the ugly and the beautiful, the hurtful and the helpful, the wanted and the unwanted, and magic or no magic. To think that you are an open door letting in whatever you are focusing on puts in perspective where your focal point needs to be. What will you be more open to? What do you want to let into your life?

Open - Where it all starts!

 ay 25

IN ORDER TO stop judging yourself and others, you have to be open to realize when you judge and be willing to practice a non-judgmental way of being and living. How will you shift yourself to walk your walk as an *open to all* kind of person, and spread that abundantly?

Open - Where it all starts!

 ay 26

BEING flexible means that you are open in your whole being; in your physical body with letting in health, in your mind with practicing positive and happy thoughts, in your soul by aligning with who you really are, and in consciousness through being one with all. How can you be more flexible—BE and live as an open energy?

___

Open - Where it all starts!

 Day 27

WHEN YOU ARE relaxed you are wide open—nothing is closed or blocked in you, for you, or as you. Breathe into this fact! Can you feel the absence of resistance or pressure in this allowing state? How will you consciously relax and make that open-ness your natural state?

Open - Where it all starts!

 ay 28

Enjoying a happy life shows that you are open to experiencing bliss—otherwise, you would not have such fun. Sounds simple, yet sometimes it is challenging because we glue our happiness to the circumstances instead of the willing-ness to just be happy no matter what. How open are you to just being happy? How will you overcome your closed-ness to feel good? Now can you make yourself even wider to allow double the joy to carry you through your days?

Open - Where it all starts!

 ay 29

IT TAKES courage to trust in life and leave it the way it is. It also takes your open-ness to give your courage and trust the power they deserve. How will you give up the fight and, instead, let your boldness and knowing rule your world?

___

Open - Where it all starts!

 ay 30

ARE you looking for more adventures—small or big? How can you be more open to adventurous experiences in your life? What steps could you take to fly freely, openly, and be more excited about you being alive?

Open - Where it all starts!

 Day 31

THINKING and feeling like a strong person means you align with that strong part in you—and yes, everyone has it! Are you open enough to override your disbelief or distrust in your unlimited strength? Look around and see all the strength in everything and everyone—write down how that force feels! Then, sense into every organ in your body and feel their strength—write down how that feels! Now that you have shifted into the essence of strength, feel your own unique energy that screams nothing but power. That is you! Journal, strong one, journal!

Open - Where it all starts!

# Day 32

LIFE IS AN EVER-CHANGING experience that is always creating new openings for you, be it in your physicality or as your energetic essence. What openings are offered to you right now? Is it a new inspiration, hobby, job, or place to live? Or is it new ways of thinking—a new alignment with your inner being? I know, it asks of your full open-ness to experience these opportunities, but you can do it!

Open - Where it all starts!

 Day 33

Respecting everything and everyone asks for an open heart that is willing to love no matter what, and requires an open view of *all* of life. Could you start with yourself and respect yourself more? How about others? How can you openly approve of everything and everyone without questioning anything or anyone?

Open - Where it all starts!

 Day 34

Your NOW is always in the open—willing to give you everything it has. Sticking consciously with your NOW by being mindful of what is present at any given moment means that you are open. How will you focus on your NOW more often? Can you indulge in this always present open-ness with a little deeper enthusiasm?

___

Open - Where it all starts!

 ay 35

OPENING YOUR HEART WIDE, and continuing to expand it as life goes on, means that you are capable of loving everything and everyone—even if that is only on your perceptional level and not necessarily practiced as a hugging-action. What would *love it all* mean for you? How can you stay lovingly open?

___

Open - Where it all starts!

 ay 36

DECIDING that today is your best day ever requests for you to be open to whatever the day has in store for you—while constantly being and living in the essence of finding the best in everything. Are you willing to do that? How will you accomplish this state of bliss?

Open - Where it all starts!

 ay 37

AS AN ENERGETIC BEING in an energetic world, unlimited energy is constantly flowing through you. Given, that's only if you are open! Are you open? How do you know when you are open? How does it feel, your super open-ness? What are your plans to stay open, and to open even more?

Open - Where it all starts!

Day 38

IMAGINE BEING A PROFESSIONAL *OPENER*—OPENING doors or gates, opening mail, opening boxes, opening the fridge, opening your eyes, opening gifts, opening your shoes, opening a treasure box. Yes, I definitely know that you are an already trained *opener*! How will you use your expertise to your advantage and consciously align with all these opening acts—to shift your whole being to BE and live as openly as you can?

_____
_____
_____
_____
_____
_____
_____
_____
_____
_____
_____
_____
_____
_____
_____
_____
_____
_____
_____
_____

Open - Where it all starts!

 Day 39

LIVING with gratitude demands for you to be open enough to see what you can be thankful for—even if it is a tiny little grain of salt. Without that broad-mindedness not much would ever stick on your gratitude board. How can you expand your appreciation-net to fish for even more goodness to find?

Open - Where it all starts!

 ay 40

AN OPEN-MINDED BEING has the ability to see, feel, hear, and live beyond what things look like in physicality. They also find and give unlimited praise to themselves, others, and happenings in life—no matter the circumstances. What compliments can you creatively come up with, especially when it seems that there is nothing to praise? List please!

Open - Where it all starts!

 ay 41

PICK the most open sight that you have available right now. A wide open door, the open ocean, the unlimited sky, or even an open candy bar will do. Focus on that open-ness—how does it feel? What do you see? What are you waiting for, become one with this open energy!

_____
_____
_____
_____
_____
_____
_____
_____
_____
_____
_____
_____
_____
_____
_____
_____
_____
_____
_____
_____

Open - Where it all starts!

 ay 42

SOMETIMES YOUR PAST has you in its grip and we all know how that feels. To let what was be, and to move on fresh and new, your infinite open-ness to forget and forgive has to be in your heart—and be your strict focus. What in your past will you let go of? And how big of an open space for new magic will that create?

___

Open - Where it all starts!

 ay 43

CHIT-CHATTING with your physical body might have others scratching their heads. But how can you do it, anyways? Not straying away from being creatively open to have constructive meetings and hear what exactly it is that your body needs and wants?

Open - Where it all starts!

 ay 44

YOU ARE a big and bright light when aligned with who you really are. Opening yourself up to your truth and the reasons of why you are here - which is to live as YOU - means that you shine brighter than one can imagine. What is your light for you? What color is it, and how big and bright does it want to be? What openness is asked of you in order to glow?

Open - Where it all starts!

 ay 45

WHEN LIFE GETS you in ways that you don't like, retrospectively, what were you open to—what did you let in? Was your focus on vividly living, freedom, happiness, and bliss? Or was it on fear, being limited, distrusting, or in disbelief? How can you shift, and stay shifted, in an open-ness that serves you and nourishes your magnificent way of experiencing life—letting in the best of the best?

Open - Where it all starts!

 ay 46

TAKE any of your physical symptoms and pick the one that's most alive. Imagine opening it up - like you would a can of beans - and feeling, seeing, and hearing into the wisdom of that energetic essence. Yes, your symptoms are energy just like everything else, and it takes you being ready to experience them as such to be open to that way of living. What do you hear, feel, and see in your opened up symptom? What is it guiding you to do?

Open - Where it all starts!

 ay 47

KINDNESS AND NICENESS are essences that are in a frequency of open-ness—open to love, peace, and joy. Being kind and nice proves that you are open, having an open heart and mind, because if you would be closed the energy or inspiration to be kind and nice would be lacking. Question is, which one comes first; you opening up to kindness or kindness opening up to you? It's a chicken and egg scenario… Fact is that the kinder you are, the more open you are—and the more open you are, the more kindness you attract. I say take the initiative, get on the kindness-train, and make your kind list!

Open - Where it all starts!

 ay 48

How would an open-ness inspired day look like for you? How will you, as an advocate for open-ness, BE and live? What will you wear, eat, listen to, hear, say, do, and indulge in? How can you make sure that you are focusing on being open, then more open, and even more open, with no end?

_____
_____
_____
_____
_____
_____
_____
_____
_____
_____
_____
_____
_____
_____
_____
_____
_____
_____
_____
_____

Open - Where it all starts!

 ay 49

To think that negativity - and everything in the field of that lower frequency - is an immediate closing of yourself and the good stuff-pipe, it makes sense to create a focused plan to stay positive—to BE and live open. What's your plan?

___

Open - Where it all starts!

 ay 50

YOU HAVE to be open to make the world go round for yourself—be the open portal that lets in unlimited amounts of health, abundance, happiness, change, betterment, and fun in life. That's where it all starts! Why? Because *closed* won't let all of the magic in and life will be tuned way down. Are you open to putting your thoughts in writing—and coming up with ways to let more light in?

Open - Where it all starts!

 ay 51

ARE you playful enough to look at your life through children glasses for a while—living in lightness and ease, while being in wonder and awe about the world and why you are here? Are you open to such a fun experience? Make your play-list here!

Open - Where it all starts!

 ay 52

HAVING a low threshold shifts you to be weak so why not change into a high threshold and be strong? Being open to everything that seems hard - differences, situations, traumas, or bad days - means you have a high threshold to conquer life with strength. Being open to all the magic - happiness, easiness, health, abundance, playfulness, and joy - means you have a high threshold to enjoy life with full force. I say, be in awe and wonder about everything you don't know, agree with, or understand, and enjoy the flexible you that you become by doing so. Are you game? If so, how will you do that?

___

Open - Where it all starts!

 ay 53

AN OPEN BEING IS A ____ being! Fill in the blank with the most flowing word and write about what that means for you? How do you feel as such? Limitless, in the flow, peaceful, resistance-free, pressure-free, or at ease? How can you shift yourself into the frequency of *open* and flow with it more often?

_____
_____
_____
_____
_____
_____
_____
_____
_____
_____
_____
_____
_____
_____
_____
_____
_____
_____
_____
_____

Open - Where it all starts!

 ay 54

ARE you open to thoughts like: I am constantly transitioning—coming into my life from pure positive energy, always changing while living my life, then transitioning from life back into pure positive energy? What do these words initiate in you? Do you feel the calm that sits in this open acceptance; that you are a transition-er and energetically never will be gone?

Open - Where it all starts!

 Day 55

TO ACCEPT everything and everyone takes your full and wide open-ness to give credences to all. How will you make this your lifestyle, and focus on accepting all as-is?

___

Open - Where it all starts!

ay 56

Who's this new open me and what have I done with my old closed self? That is the question you want to be able to ask yourself after putting in so much sweat-work to be more open—because you made a huge shift to being wide open. From there, ask yourself: What are my new true colors, what gets me excited, what makes me mad; how do I want to BE and live now? Write down your new open-minded answers and enjoy ripping off your chains.

Open - Where it all starts!

 Day 57

PURE GENEROSITY ASKS for you to be spontaneously open—to give no matter what - or how much - you have, not mind who you give to, never ask what they use it for, and to not care about whether it's day or night. Are you that open? Can you give, give, and give some more? What are you going to give so openly? Love, smiles, kindness, food, money, clothes, or even safety?

___

Open - Where it all starts!

 Day 58

Saying, feeling, hearing, tasting, smelling, and thinking the words "Thank you!" are a guaranteed opening of your heart and mind—an automatic alignment with your soul. The essence of these words are of love, light, peace, and graciousness. They are clearly high-for-life and you want to use them a million times every new day. Who's going to hear them from you? Hint, hint, starting with yourself is worth gold!

Open - Where it all starts!

 ay 59

ARE the rules you live by of an opening or closing nature for yourself and others? Do they open the space for possibilities, opportunities, love, and understanding, or are they limiting your experience of a spectacular life? Make your rule-list and sort them into two buckets—one labeled *opening*, the other *closing*. I'm sure you can guess which bucket to throw out!

___

Open - Where it all starts!

 ay 60

BEING OPENLY passionate to whatever gets your heart singing feels like ____ ! Fill in the blank and don't be surprised if your word equals "heavenly." Then make your passion list and let your heart sing!

Open - Where it all starts!

 Day 61

ARE you open to all the joy-messages that are there for you? Do you see the leaf blowing around initiating playfulness, the chirping birds bringing music to your ears, the sun creating warmth for you, the moon awakening your wishes and dreams, smiles pointed at you and making you smile too—and all other wonderful uplifts that are present for you? Are you open for this magic, wisdom, and guidance?

Open - Where it all starts!

 ay 62

WHAT IS it that you really, really, really want in your life right now? Is it a new job, a partner for life, children, money, a house, better health? Pick the one that is mostly on your mind and write it down. What does this wish feel like? Don't get hung up on its absence—instead, feel yourself into the presence of your desire. Get those wonderful feelings onto paper. Now, what kind openness is this manifestation asking of you? Is it asking for you to feel deserving, freely allow it in, and openly receive this gift? How does it feel to follow the directions and become so wonderfully open?

Open - Where it all starts!

 ay 63

THE DIVERSITY of life is an invitation to practice having an open mind—one that I hope you will take to heart because otherwise you'll go through life constantly negativing or judging yourself, others, or happenings. A clear closing up! How can you practice your mind into being - or being even more - open, all while having a good laugh here and there?

Open - Where it all starts!

 Day 64

An open being is a ___ being! Fill in the blank with the most flowing word and write about what that means for you. How do you feel as such? Limitless, in the flow, peaceful, resistance-free, pressure-free, or at ease? How can you shift yourself into the frequency of *open* and flow with it more often?

___

Open - Where it all starts!

 ay 65

EMOTIONS ARE an eye-opener keeping you on your tippy toes if you don't come to peace with the fact that they are all part of you and belong to living this wonderful life. Once embraced, your eyes stay wide open and will magically see more clearly. How clearly do you see, and how cuddly are you with your feelings?

Open - Where it all starts!

 ay 66

ONCE UPON A TIME, the comfort zone that you are in right now was created by you being open to go bigger, wider, and deeper. In order for your next new zone to be created - or even better, to explode all zones and become completely free - it takes an even bigger open-ness. Are you ready to explode? How open can you get?

Open - Where it all starts!

 ay 67

DAY-DREAMS and the art of day-dreaming are a rapid and guaranteed shift and lift into your high-for-life frequency of your newest world—one that you adore and wish for. Practicing this opens your energetic essence, which is the biggest part of you—the one that has the say, does what it wants to do, and controls you feeling well or unwell. Knowing that, how much will you go day-dreaming? How big and bold can your dreams be? Good, now go even bigger and bolder!

Open - Where it all starts!

 ay 68

SERVING the world openly creates a ton of goodness and sets the expectations of the ones serving, and all that are served, to a higher and better level—which is a great thing because expectations set the tone for manifestations. How much more open to serving yourself and others can you get? Make your *I serve openly* plan here!

Open - Where it all starts!

Day 69

IMAGINE A LIFE FILLED WITH DRAMA—SOME is yours and some is not. Feel how dense you get and the closed-ness to happiness, good solutions, and magic this creates. Now feel yourself into a drama free life and sense how relaxed, free, and light this feels—how open you get. Make your "shoot these dramas to the moon" list here!

___

Open - Where it all starts!

 ay 70

Do you love feeling blessed? Do you enjoy blessings? Do you like blessing others with wonderful gestures, words, things, or gifts? Of course that's a "YES!" because it feels so incredibly good, and means that you are wide open. What blessings are you going to give? Which ones are you going to receive, and how will you focus on feeling blessed all day long? Go for a bountiful goodness journal entry here.

Open - Where it all starts!

 ay 71

I WANT to hear what gifts you have! Tell me openly and freely about what they are, how they make you feel, what gives them a spark, and how you express them in your life. Please be really open with me! Kind Regards, your journal.

Open - Where it all starts!

# Day 72

THINKING that the impossible is actually very possible asks for you to be open to the fact that everything is energy, and that you are in charge of your life and the manifestations in it—as long as you put your focus on aligning with its frequency you can have whatever you want. Are you open to this way of living? Can you blindly trust in such good news? How does this feel and look for you, this empowered life of yours?

Open - Where it all starts!

 ay 73

YOU ALWAYS HAVE choices in life! Now imagine that one of them is a wild one but feels amazing. What would keep you from going for it, even though you feel that it would be the right one? Is it the wildness? List all your *whats* and *whys*, know that those are your blockages—ready to be opened wide so that next time, you can decide from a wide open *you*. Enjoy the clarity this creates!

Open - Where it all starts!

 ay 74

WHAT DOES the most open version of you look and feel like? How do you think as that top-notch you? How does your body feel, and how do you see, taste, smell, hear, and act in life? Be very descriptive here!

___

Open - Where it all starts!

 ay 75

BEING able to take your time, and only get into the hustle when it's of a good feeling nature, needs your full trust and open-ness in knowing, believing, and having confidence in yourself that you are living your life perfectly. Hence, when it's not good, you won't hustle—instead, you will relax and align until acting is the right thing to do again. Are you that trusting and that open? How will you give yourself this wonderful break?

___

Open - Where it all starts!

 ay 76

CAN you be open enough to the belief that you are the most beautiful and gorgeous being ever? Are you willing to say this to yourself in front of the mirror until you feel the truth of it, and are you rooted enough in this open-ness to show up as such a beautiful and gorgeous essence—to BE and live your life beautifully and gorgeously? I know, sometimes it takes effort, but you can do it!

Open - Where it all starts!

 ay 77

BASING your enjoyment of life on appreciating even the smallest particle of your life creates an open field of mindfulness in which your heart can fill up with gentle energy. Try it! Feel appreciation for a grain of salt, a crystal of sugar, or a kernel of rice because these tiny little things have unlimited magic for you. Journal, wise one, journal!

Open - Where it all starts!

Day 78

CONSCIOUSNESS IS AN OPEN FIELD! To the naked eye it looks empty and like a space of nothing—yet, scientists say it is filled with information and wisdom. Being always one with, and staying connected to, such a grand open-ness is naturally of well-feeling nature because you'll always have access to the knowledge and will never be alone. Feel yourself into consciousness—how is that for you? How will you become one with this open field and also stay focused as such?

Open - Where it all starts!

 Day 79

THE BIGGEST PART of you - your inner you - is something that you can't physically grab or hold, and sometimes it doesn't even make sense on the physical life level. Many times you are open to hearing it loud and clear whereas other times you are closed, deaf. Yet, it is always there. How can you be more persistent to staying open and hearing it clearly—aligning with your energetic you?

Open - Where it all starts!

 ay 80

TO FEEL deserving means that you need to be open enough to know your enormous value, to feel and see your magic, and to accept, respect, thank, and love yourself without rules or conditions attached. Sounds like unconditional love! How will you be wide open to your ultimate worthiness? Can you love yourself freely and fully?

Open - Where it all starts!

 ay 81

WHAT OLD SAYINGS - or thoughts - that you practice are closing you down, and will you replace those with words that make you feel happy and open you up? For inspiration's sake, here are some opening statements: "Life is easy peasy!" "I have plenty of time for everything!" "I am limitless!" "Life loves me!" "I am always supported!" "I am OK, everything is OK!"

Open - Where it all starts!

 ay 82

BEING LOUD, big, colorful, crazy, wild, unique, and vivid takes some real boldness sometimes—but even more truthfully, it takes your complete open-ness to BE and live yourself fully and unquestionably. Once open you don't need to be bold anymore because you'll be too busy enjoying, laughing, and having fun. What does your quirky *you* look, feel, and act like? Go wild here!

Open - Where it all starts!

 ay 83

TAKING time to do nothing else than being present with the little things in life - the ones that are normal, and a given - opens you up to all kind of high-for-life moments. What teeny-tinyness in your surroundings right now can you be present with? How will you create more of these tiny-NOW moments?

Open - Where it all starts!

 ay 84

THINK of a sandal versus a hiking boot! The open shoe is worn when it's sunny, warm, dry, and pleasantly safe for your toes to shine their light bright, all while letting in the goodness that's there. The closed shoe you wear when things get rough—keeping all that's there out. Clearly, one lets in and out, like an exchange, while the other keeps it all in but also out—no exchange. I want you to BE and live like a sandal more often! How will you live in exchange with the universe—letting in more magic to shine your light brighter towards the world?

Open - Where it all starts!

 ay 85

COMPLAINTS AND COMPLAINING closes you automatically to the good that wants to move into your life, whereas praising opens up the pipes for the greatest of things, feelings, and happenings to arrive without doubt. How will you stop yourself from complaining, and instead, shift into the frequency of compliments?

Open - Where it all starts!

 ay 86

SPENDING time in someone else's garden is a nice visit but at some point it's great to go home. If overstayed it becomes exhausting for the visitor and the owner—not to mention that if the guest turns the visit into a weeding activity it creates friction. That shift from fun to doom means the energy just went from being open to closed, for both the invitee and the host. How will you stay more in your own life, only visiting other people's business if it's right, returning home when it's time, and keep from fixing things unless it's yourself?

Open - Where it all starts!

 Day 87

BEING spontaneous means that you are open to having a good time! What are you waiting for, and what spontaneity will you follow openly and blindly today?

Open - Where it all starts!

 ay 88

BEING SERIOUS OFTEN, and about most of the happenings in life, is a guaranteed switch to being closed. Why? Because it takes the open-ness of laughter, fun, light-ness, and joy out of the equation and those light-hearted energies are needed in order to be wide open to a vivid life. I say, amuse and be amused more often—open-up more often! How will you do that?

Open - Where it all starts!

Day 89

THE IMAGINATION IS an opening tool to live a creative and phenomenal life because it shifts you to BE and live in your desired wish-frequency. So, are you open enough to imagine yourself as a superhero? Why? Because a superhero is limitless and energized to the extent of an *out-of-this-world* energy—and your inner being is an *out-of-this-world* and limitless energy, making your biggest part of you equal to a superhero. Write, superhero, write about that!

Open - Where it all starts!

 ay 90

SPEAKING OF SUPER HERO! You have to decide: What is your super power? Be very widely open here—open to more, to bigger, to better, to grander, and to unlimited power!

_____
_____
_____
_____
_____
_____
_____
_____
_____
_____
_____
_____
_____
_____
_____
_____
_____
_____
_____

Open - Where it all starts!

* * *

Ready to continue on your self-growth path? Get the next journal in this series: ***To BE and Live - The reason you are here!***

BONUS

Because hey, nobody ever wants the goodness to end.

Keep on opening!

 Day 91

ALL YOUR SYMPTOMS - PHYSICAL, emotional, and energetic - are profound growing opportunities for you. The growth sits right in the middle of embracing and feeling them. Are you open to allowing yourself to fall in love with your symptoms, and also following their guidance?

_____
_____
_____
_____
_____
_____
_____
_____
_____
_____
_____
_____
_____
_____
_____
_____
_____
_____
_____
_____
_____
_____
_____
_____

Open - Where it all starts!

 ay 92

WHAT DO you want right now and how will you open up to receiving it? Make your *I-want-list* here!

Open - Where it all starts!

 ay 93

BEING and living high-for-life is a state of open-ness—one that represents what you said you would do when you decided to come into your physicality. The ups and downs, and lefts and rights, are also part of that state—however, you promised yourself to BE and live in the open-ness of love while handling them. How will you claim your full open-ness, even in hard times, and fulfill your promise to yourself?

___

Open - Where it all starts!

 Day 94

N<small>AY-SAYERS</small>, negative-ers, and down-ers are closed to the full magic of being alive. So why would you even entangle yourself with them—closing yourself too? How will you stay in your magic, no matter if others have closed themselves and are walking closed through their lives?

Open - Where it all starts!

 ay 95

WHAT OPEN-NESS WOULD you act on if nobody would be watching? Might be a silly - or even dangerous - question, but I had to ask, and since this is your journal you can get really really truthful here. Go for it!

Open - Where it all starts!

AND NOW IT'S YOUR TURN!

The following are your magical pages to turn your own personal closed-ness into being open.

I'm counting on you to go wide here!

ay 96

OPEN-NESS IS...

Open - Where it all starts!

 ay 97

OPEN-NESS IS...

Open - Where it all starts!

 ay 98

Open-ness is...

___

Open - Where it all starts!

 Day 99

Open-ness is...

Open - Where it all starts!

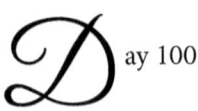ay 100

OPEN-NESS IS...

Open - Where it all starts!

ALSO BY JACQUELINE PIRTLE

365 Days of Happiness

Because happiness is a piece of cake!

This passage book invites you to create a daily habit to live your every day joy, and is the parent companion to *365 Days of Happiness*, the journal workbook.

* * *

365 Days of Happiness - Special Edition

Because happiness is a piece of cake

This beautiful Special Edition of the bestseller *365 Days of Happiness: Because happiness is a piece of cake* has room for your notes after every daily passage.

* * *

365 Days of Happiness - **Journal Workbook**

This enlightening journal workbook is your daily tool to create a habit of living your every day bliss, and is the companion to *365 Days of Happiness: Because happiness is a piece of cake*.

* * *

Life IS Beautiful - Here's to New Beginnings

If you like digging deeper into the meaning of life and are inspired by spirituality, then you'll love Jacqueline's effective teachings.

* * *

Parenting Through the Eyes of Lollipops

A Guide to Conscious Parenting

If you like harmony at home and laughter in the house, then you'll love Jacqueline's inspirational methods.

* * *

What it Means to BE a Woman

And Yes! Women do Poop!

If you like to live free, empowered, and want to decide for yourself, then you'll love Jacqueline's liberating ways.

* * *

What. If. - A 30 Day Journal

Turning your what IFs into it IS!

If you like to be in charge of your own life, turn your dreams into reality, enjoy journaling, and want to squeeze the most out of your time, then you'll love Jacqueline uplifting teachings.

* * *

What. If. - A 90 Day Journal - The Extended Edition

Turning your what IFs into it IS!

If you like to be in charge of your own life, turn your dreams into reality, enjoy journaling, and want to squeeze the most out of your time, then you'll love Jacqueline uplifting teachings.

ABOUT THE AUTHOR

Bestselling author, podcaster, and holistic practitioner, Jacqueline Pirtle, has twenty-four years of experience helping thousands of clients discover their own happiness. Jacqueline is the owner of **FreakyHealer** and has shared her solid teachings through her podcast **The Daily Freak**, sessions, workshops, presentations, and books with clients all over the world. She holds international degrees in holistic health and natural living. Her effective healing work has been featured in print and online magazines, podcasts, radio shows, on TV, and in the documentary *The Overly Emotional Child by Learning Success*, available on Amazon Prime.

For any questions you might have, to sign up for Jacqueline's newsletter, and for more information on whatever else she is up to, visit www.freakyhealer.com and her social media accounts @freakyhealer.

www.ingramcontent.com/pod-product-compliance
Lightning Source LLC
Chambersburg PA
CBHW071420070526
44578CB00003B/630